CHICKEN WINGS
AND 99 OTHER SEMI PROVEN FACTS

BRUCE A. VEACH

An8ther Hours Publishing

Published by Another 8 Hours Publishing
O'Fallon, Illinois
http://www.Another8Hours.com

Photography: © Tracey Allen
Cover Design and Interior Layout: Another 8 Hours, Inc.

Copyright © 2013 by Bruce A Veach.
All rights reserved.

No part of this book may be reproduced or utilized in any form, by any means, electronic or mechanical, including photocopying and recording, or by any information storage and retrieval system, without permission in writing from the author.

ISBN, print ed. 978-0-9828585-6-1

First Printing May 2013
Printed in United States of America

Acknowledgements

This book is dedicated to the people in my life who made it possible.

My mother and father, Mary and Carl
Who allowed me to be me and did not stifle my creativity.

My daughters, Mariellen and Kelly
Who provide me with inspiration everyday and are easily the greatest accomplishment I will have while on this earth.

My best friend, Shelbie
You are one of the few people in my life who supported all my crazy ideas. Nobody could ask for a more supportive and caring friend than you. Because of your encouragement and inspiration I am truly blessed. You, my friend, are indeed a princess.

Special Recognition to my college buddy Laura Angelus for contributing semi-proven fact Number 11

Foreword

Dr. Jim Guinee is a licensed psychologist and adjunct professor at the University of Central Arkansas. Jim and Slat have been friends over 30 years, but not in a row. He is a huge fan of comics, and a huge fan of THIS huge comic.

Dull. Serious. Unimaginative.

These are three words that no one ever ascribes to Bruce "Slat" Veach. I think it's safe to say that had I not met and befriended him in college, my experiences would have been far less interesting. I think *anyone* who comes across his path shares this sentiment.

How shall I describe my rotund friend? He reminds me of a children's song... incessantly charming, inherently silly, and in the end the cause of mental anguish and strangulation.

As a psychologist, I have always been fascinated with (and somewhat envious of) comedians. They stand on a stage, grasp a cold microphone, and warmly recall everyday life events with amazing clarity and hilarity. The *really* good ones, like Slat, go further and make unique observations about life that leave the rest of us wondering *where in the world did he come up with that*?

Where *does* Slat come up with his observations about life? Simple. They originate in that infantile brain of his. Like the rest of him, his brain will never grow up. It will remain a child's brain. And like all children, he will observe life in a wondrous and weird way. Those of us who are fortunate enough to be around him will just wonder.

Years ago I wrote a yet to be published novel recalling my fraternity days at the University of Illinois. The few who have read my book have all asked the same question: is Slat a real person? *Are you kidding me*? I couldn't create someone like him if I tried.

I can only promise that everything I am about to write about him is based on fact. Allow me to share a small sample of Slat, a series of what I call "It was Slat"…

It was Slat who encouraged me to greet every college coed as a "young American goddess of fertility."

It was Slat who couldn't get up for a 10am college class but every Saturday rose before 8am to start his "cartoon marathon."

It was Slat who would pretend to spot a strange object in the sky, draw a crowd of students around him, and then walk away while the crowd continued to wonder what they were supposed to be looking at.

It was Slat whose car died in the Burger King drive-thru, only to insist we push it up to the speaker so that "we can place our order before the tow truck gets here."

It was Slat who created a radio program called "*The Men from Scrod*" about two aliens who were spawned from a cosmic egg solely for the purpose of removing Boy George from the airwaves.

It was Slat who set the goal of stealing my camera and taking pictures of himself so that every roll had at least one mug shot.

It was Slat who inspired our first fraternity party, simply because cable television had been installed in the house that afternoon. The theme? *Ode to Cable*

It was Slat who almost put a quick end to that same party when he managed to kick some sorority girl in the head while showing her a dance move. Later that night he refused to come out of his room, hollering, "And I don't have that girl naked in my closet!"

It was Slat who bought a parakeet and named him "Goober," and then kept him in the darkened basement of the fraternity until Goober began hanging *upside down on his perch*.

It was Slat who emerged one afternoon from happy hour, drunk, and marched onto the front lawn of the fraternity with the largest population of athletes, challenging them to a wrestling match—a*ll of them at once.*

It was Slat who got *really* drunk and tried to drive to his ex-girlfriend's apartment, forcing me to climb onto his car to keep him from doing so. But not before he tried to dislodge me from his car hood by turning on the windshield wipers and wiper fluid.

It was Slat who came running into the fraternity house one afternoon and excitedly announced a local pizza place had a hot air balloon over campus, dropping free pizzas. I chased that damn hot air balloon halfway across campus before I realized I'd been had.

It was Slat who assembled a small army of students for an Illini hockey game, sat above the opposing team's bench, and taunted them so much the goalie saved the puck *and then threw it at Slat*.

It was Slat who inspired the fraternity's annual scavenger hunt, but rigged each one so most of the items could be found in the trunk of his Buick.

It was Slat who inserted the word "aforementioned" into every essay he ever wrote in college.

It was also Slat who wrote an essay for a fellow classmate (to repay a debt), arguing that "old people are useless and should be eliminated from society," in an effort to thoroughly shock their teacher. Yet it was Slat who was shocked when this essay received praise from their instructor for its "bold opinions," *earning a higher grade than the paper he wrote for himself.*

It was Slat, a scholastic underachiever (that's being kind), who managed to get himself elected president of the fraternity, a fraternity that consistently boasted the *highest grade point average on campus.*

It was Slat who once organized a food fight in our dorm cafeteria as a means of protesting the quality of food, and yet managed to escape being punished because he never lifted a finger *except to raise his umbrella.*

It was Slat who found himself one night besieged by his fraternity brothers, armed with snowballs, and managed to escape an all-out assault by disappearing into the bushes and later jumping out of a pizza delivery truck and into his car.

It was Slat who once invited a Jewish girl to the fraternity house for lunch and served her pork rinds.

It was Slat who stood outside a local movie theater and actually tried to convince people he was Tom Cruise. *In a few cases he actually succeeded.*

So...enjoy this book from my favorite comedian from Shiloh, Illinois. Take a little piece of Slat home with you. As you can see, there's plenty more where it came from.

P.S. Bruce's middle name is Adrian!

NUMBER 1.

FOLKS LOVE CHICKEN WINGS.

NUMBER 2.

BABIES LOVE TO BE NAKED.

2 | FOLKS LOVE CHICKEN WINGS

NUMBER 3.

GOOD THINGS HAPPEN WHEN YOU SHOOT FROM THE POINT.

NUMBER 4.

DESPITE THE FACT IT ISN'T: "FUNNEST" SHOULD BE A WORD.

NUMBER 5.

THE BOUNCE PASS IS BAD.

FOLKS LOVE CHICKEN WINGS

NUMBER 6.

> THE KEY TO GOOD PORK AND BEANS IS THE BEANS, NOT SO MUCH THE PORK.

NUMBER 7.

NO MATTER WHERE YOU GO IN THIS COUNTRY YOU WILL SEE THE WORLD'S LARGEST FIREWORK STAND.

NUMBER 8.

IF YOU WANT TO RUIN A GREAT IDEA, INVOLVE OTHER PEOPLE.

NUMBER 9.

THERE ISN'T A WOMAN IN THE WORLD THAT CAN'T FIND 10 THINGS WRONG WITH HER.

NUMBER 10.

THERE ISN'T A MAN ALIVE WHO DOESN'T THINK HE IS PERFECT.

FOLKS LOVE CHICKEN WINGS

NUMBER 11.

A TOWN'S "TOURISTINESS" IS DIRECTLY PROPORTIONATE TO THE NUMBER OF FUDGE SHOPS IT HAS.

NUMBER 12.

YOU DON'T REALIZE HOW MUCH YOUR PARENTS LOVED YOU UNTIL YOU SIT THROUGH YOUR 12 YEAR OLD CHILD'S BAND CONCERT.

12 | FOLKS LOVE CHICKEN WINGS

NUMBER 13.

THERE ISN'T A MALE UNDER THE AGE OF 10, WHO, WHEN GIVEN A GARDEN HOSE, WONT EVENTUALLY PUT IT DOWN HIS PANTS.

NUMBER 14.

IT IS FAR EASIER TO GAIN WEIGHT THAN TO LOSE WEIGHT.

NUMBER 15.

IF YOU'RE IN A HURRY, YOU WILL END UP BEHIND SOMEONE WHO HAS ALL DAY AND ACTS LIKE IT.

NUMBER 16.

MOST PEOPLE WHO HUNT AREN'T TOLSTOY ENTHUSIASTS.

NUMBER 17.

IT IS MUCH BETTER TO HAVE A BEST FRIEND AND A FEW CLOSE FRIENDS THAN IT IS TO HAVE A WHOLE BUNCH OF ACQUAINTANCES.

NUMBER 18.

WHEN THE QUESTION IS "DO YOU WANT FRIES WITH THAT?" THE ANSWER IS SELDOM: YES.

NUMBER 19.

WHEN USING A PUBLIC RESTROOM, YOU SHOULD CHECK FOR TOILET PAPER BEFORE YOU SIT DOWN.

NUMBER 20.

THE OLDER A MAN GETS, THE MORE HE ENJOYS A SHIRT POCKET.

NUMBER 21.

NO MATTER HOW MUCH MONEY YOU MAKE, IT IS GENERALLY NOT ENOUGH.

NUMBER 22.

PEOPLE REMEMBER BAD THINGS MUCH LONGER THAN THEY REMEMBER GOOD THINGS.

NUMBER 23.

THERE ARE 208 WEEKS IN A 4-YEAR PERIOD. FOR 206 OF THEM, MOST AMERICANS COULD CARE LESS ABOUT GYMNASTICS.

NUMBER 24.

> THERE ISN'T A 2 1/2 TO 10 YEAR OLD ALIVE THAT THE MENTION OF BEDTIME DOESN'T INVOKE THE SENSATION OF THIRST.

FOLKS LOVE CHICKEN WINGS

NUMBER 25.

WHEN YOU ARE BETWEEN THE AGES OF 13 AND 23 YOUR PARENTS ARE IDIOTS; WHEN YOU HIT 24, IT IS AMAZING HOW MUCH YOUR PARENTS HAVE LEARNED.

NUMBER 26.

NEVER FIGHT A TWO FRONTED WAR IN ASIA.

NUMBER 27.

A SURE FIRE WAY TO PUT YOURSELF IN A BAD MOOD IS TO GO RENEW YOUR DRIVER'S LICENSE.

NUMBER 28.

TACO BELL WILL SELDOM GET YOUR ORDER RIGHT AT THE DRIVE THRU.

NUMBER 29.

THERE'S A REASON THE FOUNDING FATHERS SAID YOU HAVE TO BE 35 YEARS OLD TO RUN FOR PRESIDENT.

NUMBER 30.

PEOPLE GENERALLY WAIT TOO LONG TO TELL OTHERS WHAT THEY MEAN TO THEM.

30 | FOLKS LOVE CHICKEN WINGS

NUMBER 31.

IT'S HARD TO BE IN A BAD MOOD WITH A HERSHEY'S KISS IN YOUR MOUTH.

NUMBER 32.

"SHOWGIRLS" IS THE WORST MOVIE YOU'LL WATCH 47 TIMES.

NUMBER 33.

THE MAIN REASON TECHNOLOGY KEEPS ADVANCING IS NOT TO MAKE LIFE EASIER, BUT RATHER SO CHILDREN CAN FEEL SMARTER THAN THEIR PARENTS.

NUMBER 34.

ORANGE IS THE WORST PRIMARY UNIFORM COLOR.

NUMBER 35.

THERE ARE 3 THINGS THAT MAKE MOST FOOD BETTER; HOT SAUCE, GRAVY, AND CHEESE.

NUMBER 36.

THERE ARE MANY GREAT MEN AND WOMEN IN THIS COUNTRY THAT WOULD MAKE GOOD LEADERS. THEY JUST DON'T RUN FOR OFFICE.

NUMBER 37.

NOTHING MOTIVATES YOU TO LOSE WEIGHT LIKE AN UPCOMING REUNION.

NUMBER 38.

MOST PEOPLE ARE QUICK TO JUDGE AND SLOW TO FORGET.

38 FOLKS LOVE CHICKEN WINGS

NUMBER 39.

WHEN YOU'RE IN HIGH SCHOOL, IF YOU ARE DATING SOMEONE FROM A DIFFERENT SCHOOL THAT AUTOMATICALLY MAKES YOU COOLER.

NUMBER 40.

A CHILD WILL NEVER LOVE THEIR PARENT AS MUCH AS THE PARENT LOVES THE CHILD, AND THAT'S ALRIGHT.

NUMBER 41.

THE PRICE OF GAS GOES UP MUCH QUICKER THAN IT COMES BACK DOWN.

NUMBER 42.

YOU WOULD BE HARD PRESSED TO FIND A BETTER BEVERAGE THAN A SLURPEE.

FOLKS LOVE CHICKEN WINGS

NUMBER 43.

THE MICROWAVE DOES NOT MAKE FOR A GOOD CLOTHES DRYER.

NUMBER 44.

KELLY TRIPUCKA IS THE MOST UNDERRATED BASKETBALL PLAYER OF ALL TIME.

44 | FOLKS LOVE CHICKEN WINGS

NUMBER 45.

> YOU CAN DO EVERYTHING YOU WANT IN LIFE. YOU JUST CAN'T DO IT ALL AT ONE TIME.

NUMBER 46.

THE BEST MOVIE EVER MADE IS "THE SHAWSHANK REDEMPTION".

NUMBER 47.

IT IS A SAFE BET THAT 50% OF AMERICANS' WEIGHT ON THEIR DRIVERS LICENSE IS NOT WITHIN 20 LBS OF THEIR ACTUAL WEIGHT.

NUMBER 48.

WHILE NOT A BAD CONCEPT, THE TUBE TOP IS SELDOM EXECUTED PROPERLY.

NUMBER 49.

IN THE NATIONAL LEAGUE
WHEN THE OPPOSING
PITCHER GETS A HIT,
BAD THINGS USUALLY
ENSUE.

NUMBER 50.

YOU SHOULD ALWAYS SAY GOODBYE AS IF YOU ARE NEVER GOING TO SEE THAT PERSON AGAIN.

NUMBER 51.

WORKING OUT IS LIKE GIVING BIRTH.

YOU'RE NOT ENJOYING IT WHILE IT'S HAPPENING. YOU DON'T CARE WHAT YOU LOOK LIKE DURING IT, BUT WHEN IT'S OVER YOU FEEL VERY REWARDED.

NUMBER 52.

SPEND ONE DAY AT ANY GOVERNMENT AGENCY AND YOU WILL BE AMAZED THAT WE ARE STILL A FREE NATION.

NUMBER 53.

YOU ALWAYS FIND SOMETHING IN THE LAST PLACE YOU LOOKED... BECAUSE IF YOU KEEP LOOKING AFTER YOU FIND IT, YOU ARE AN IDIOT.

NUMBER 54.

WOMEN NEVER HAVE ENOUGH SHOES.

FOLKS LOVE CHICKEN WINGS

NUMBER 55.

IT IS IMPOSSIBLE FOR AN ADULT MALE TO WATCH "FIELD OF DREAMS" AND NOT CRY.

NUMBER 56.

DOCTORS SELDOM RUN AHEAD OF SCHEDULE.

FOLKS LOVE CHICKEN WINGS

NUMBER 57.

FOR ANY MALE UNDER THE AGE OF 20, CLOTHES ARE NEVER A "GOOD" GIFT.

NUMBER 58.

JUNIOR HIGH AND HIGH SCHOOL COACHES SHOULDN'T KEEP PLAYERS THEY ARE NOT GOING TO PLAY. BREAK THEIR HEARTS ONCE, NOT 20 TIMES.

NUMBER 59.

FEMALES IN THE PASSENGER SEAT OF A CAR HAVE THE ABILITY TO PLACE THEIR HEAD DIRECTLY IN THE LINE OF SIGHT OF A MALE DRIVER NEEDING TO CHECK FOR ONCOMING TRAFFIC ON THEIR RIGHT.

NUMBER 60.

THE BEST PART OF BEING IN LOVE IS FALLING IN LOVE.

60 | FOLKS LOVE CHICKEN WINGS

NUMBER 61.

GETTING MARRIED SHOULD HENCEFORTH BE REFERRED TO AS "COMMITTING MATRIMONY".

NUMBER 62.

TEACHERS DON'T SPEND ENOUGH TIME TEACHING THE PROPER USAGE OF "YOUR" AND "YOU'RE".

NUMBER 63.

IF YOU WANT TEENAGERS TO STOP HAVING SEX, HAVE THEM ALL GET MARRIED.

NUMBER 64.

THERE IS ALWAYS ONE PERSON IN EVERY GROUP OF FRIENDS THAT NO ONE IS SURE WHY THEY ARE THERE. IF YOU DON'T KNOW WHO THAT PERSON IS IN YOUR GROUP, IT'S PROBABLY YOU.

NUMBER 65.

IF YOU COULD MAKE MONEY SLEEPING; MOST TEENAGERS WOULD BE RICH.

NUMBER 66.

HIGH SCHOOL IS SIMULTANEOUSLY FOUR OF THE BEST YEARS OF YOUR LIFE WHILE BEING FOUR OF THE MOST MISERABLE YEARS OF YOUR LIFE.

NUMBER 67.

THE GREATEST BEAUTY OF OUR DEMOCRACY IS ALSO ITS GREATEST TRAGEDY. EVERYBODY CAN VOTE.

NUMBER 68.

WE OFTEN MISTAKE OUR SOUL MATE FOR OUR TRUE LOVE.

NUMBER 69.

GALS LOOK SEXY IN BASEBALL CAPS.

FOLKS LOVE CHICKEN WINGS | 69

NUMBER 70.

THE WORST SONG EVER WRITTEN IS RICHARD HARRIS' "MACARTHUR PARK" AS SUNG BY DONNA SUMMERS.

NUMBER 71.

DO THE RIGHT THING BECAUSE IT'S THE RIGHT THING TO DO. MAKE GOOD DECISIONS, BE HONEST AND GOOD THINGS WILL HAPPEN.

NUMBER 72.

MOST CHILDREN'S FAVORITE FLAVOR IS ACTUALLY A COLOR.

NUMBER 73.

THE FACT THAT MORE PEOPLE DIE FROM FALLING OFF OF DONKEYS EVERY YEAR THAN FLYING STILL DOESN'T MAKE THOSE WHO FEAR FLYING FEEL BETTER. IT JUST MAKES THEM FEAR DONKEYS.

NUMBER 74.

THOUGH MUCH MALIGNED, THE MULLET IS A GOOD LOOK.

NUMBER 75.

YOU MAY NOT ALWAYS BE RIGHT, BUT ALWAYS BE SURE.

NUMBER 76.

PHONE BOOTHS AND PHONE BOOKS WILL SOON GO THE WAY OF DINOSAURS ONLY THEY WON'T BE AS COOL.

NUMBER 77.

IF YOU ARE ON A SPORTS TEAM THAT WINS A TROPHY: GRAB THE TROPHY YOU WILL BE IN ALL THE PICTURES.

FOLKS LOVE CHICKEN WINGS

NUMBER 78.

TEENAGERS ARE INCAPABLE OF CLOSING DOORS AND DRAWERS.

NUMBER 79.

DOGS HAVE THE ABILITY TO FIND THE ONE PERSON IN THE ROOM WHO DOESN'T LIKE DOGS AND TRY TO CUDDLE WITH THEM.

NUMBER 80.

THE MOST UNDERRATED TV SHOW OF ALL TIME IS "FREAKS AND GEEKS".

80 | FOLKS LOVE CHICKEN WINGS

NUMBER 81.

AT SPORTS EVENTS AND CONCERTS, PEOPLE WHO NEED TO GO TO THE BATHROOM FREQUENTLY, ALWAYS END UP IN THE MIDDLE OF THE ROW.

NUMBER 82.

VERY SELDOM DO CHILDREN BUILD SNOWWOMEN.

FOLKS LOVE CHICKEN WINGS

NUMBER 83.

IF YOU LOVE SOMETHING SET IT FREE. OTHERWISE THERE WILL BE A SWAT TEAM OUTSIDE YOUR HOUSE PROCLAIMING THROUGH A BULLHORN "RELEASE THE WOMAN AND COME OUT WITH YOUR HANDS UP".

NUMBER 84.

PEEPS SHOULD ONLY BE SOLD AT EASTER TIME.

NUMBER 85.

IF I WAS ON DEATH ROW, MY LAST MEAL WOULD BE THE MCRIB SANDWICH, THE SHAMROCK SHAKE, AND STARBUCKS PUMPKIN SPICE LATTE. NOT BECAUSE I AM A FAN OF ANY OF THESE ITEMS, BUT RATHER BECAUSE THEY ARE ALL ONLY AVAILABLE FOR A LIMITED TIME AND SELDOM AT THE SAME TIME.

NUMBER 86.

THE ELECTORAL COLLEGE IS MORE CONFUSING THAN REGULAR COLLEGE.

NUMBER 87.

ONCE YOU'RE IN A ROUNDABOUT, DO NOT YIELD. YOU OWN THE ROUNDABOUT UNTIL YOU EXIT IT.

NUMBER 88.

IF SOMEONE SAYS THAT THEY AREN'T HIGH MAINTENANCE, THAT'S USUALLY THE FIRST CLUE THAT THEY ARE, IN FACT, HIGH MAINTENANCE.

NUMBER 89.

WHEN YOU ARE IN YOUR 20'S AND YOU WAKE UP WITH AN INK STAMP ON YOUR HAND IT MEANS YOU PROBABLY HAD A WILD NIGHT. WHEN THE SAME THING HAPPENS IN YOUR 40'S IT PROBABLY MEANS YOU HAVE AN ATHLETIC CHILD.

NUMBER 90.

IN A TOWN OF LESS THAN 8,000 PEOPLE, IF YOU CAN LOCATE THE DAIRY QUEEN, YOU PROBABLY LOCATED THE HIGH SCHOOL AS WELL.

90 | FOLKS LOVE CHICKEN WINGS

NUMBER 91.

THERE SHOULD BE A WORD TO DESCRIBE THE RESIDUE LEFT ON YOUR HANDS AFTER EATING DORITOS.

NUMBER 92.

THE WORST THING IN SPORTS IS AN OVERTIME JV GAME.

FOLKS LOVE CHICKEN WINGS

NUMBER 93.

WHEN A TRAFFIC LIGHT CHANGES FROM RED TO GREEN IT SIGNALS TO THE FIRST CAR IN LINE AT THE LIGHT TO PROCEED WITH CAUTION. IT SIGNALS TO THE SECOND CAR IN LINE TO IMMEDIATELY START HONKING AT THE FIRST CAR IN LINE.

NUMBER 94.

WHILE IT WOULD SEEM LIKE A GREAT FIT, MINIATURE GOLF WITH CHILDREN IS A NIGHTMARE.

NUMBER 95.

BEARDS AND GOATEES ARE COOL AND DISTINGUISHED. HOWEVER, JUST A MOUSTACHE IS CREEPY.

FOLKS LOVE CHICKEN WINGS

NUMBER 96.

IF I ONLY HAD 5 MINUTES TO LIVE, I WOULD WANT IT TO BE THE LAST 5 MINUTES OF AN NBA GAME.

FOLKS LOVE CHICKEN WINGS

NUMBER 97.

A HOUSE FULL OF MEN REQUIRES LESS TOILET PAPER THAN A ROOM FULL OF WOMEN.

NUMBER 98.

A FREE THROW IS THE EASIEST SHOT IN BASKETBALL. YOU ARE FIFTEEN FEET AWAY FROM A STATIONARY TARGET, YOU CAN TAKE YOUR TIME, AND NO ONE IS GUARDING YOU. IT'S EASIER THAN A LAYUP.

NUMBER 99.

WE BECOME MUCH HAPPIER PEOPLE WHEN WE STOP DWELLING ON WHAT WE CAN'T DO AND BEGIN FOCUSING ON WHAT WE CAN DO.

NUMBER 100.

PEOPLE WILL READ SILLY BOOKS.

100 | FOLKS LOVE CHICKEN WINGS

About the Author

"I just observe life and report back what I see."

Bruce Veach is a standup comic based in the Midwest. He began performing in 1985, and over the years has developed a style that truly entertains his audiences. When you come to his show, don't expect to hear one-liner after one-liner. Instead, be prepared for his unique spin on real life situations like donating blood or raising teenage daughters.

After spending his early years as a comic in traditional comedy clubs, he then performed exclusively as a Christian Comic in churches for eight years before returning to the club circuit. These church experiences armed him with the ability to have an audience rolling on the floor with laughter, without worrying about being red with embarrassment. This trait makes him perfect for any type of audience as he relies on wit and cleverness, not shock and profanity to achieve laughter.

Bruce has had the opportunity to work with the likes of Grammy Award Nominated Artist Kirk Talley, Marc Price (*Family Ties)*, Rain Pryor (*Head of the Class)*, and Dean Schardan (*Long Road Home).*

Bruceaveach@gmail.com
www.bruceveach.com